Two Coats for Joseph
The Story of Young Joseph

We are grateful to the following team of authors for their contributions to *God Loves Me*, a Bible story program for young children. This Bible story, one of a series of fifty-two, was written by Patricia L. Nederveld, managing editor for CRC Publications. Suggestions for using this book were developed by Sherry Ten Clay, training coordinator for CRC Publications and freelance author from Albuquerque, New Mexico. Yvonne Van Ee, an early childhood educator, served as project consultant and wrote *God Loves Me*, the program guide that accompanies this series of Bible storybooks.

Nederveld has served as a consultant to Title I early childhood programs in Colorado. She has extensive experience as a writer, teacher, and consultant for federally funded preschool, kindergarten, and early childhood programs in Colorado, Texas, Michigan, Florida, Missouri, and Washington, using the High/Scope Education Research Foundation curriculum. In addition to writing the Bible Footprints church school curriculum for four- and five-year-olds, Nederveld edited the revised *Threes* curriculum and the first edition of preschool through second grade materials for the *LiFE* curriculum, all published by CRC Publications.

Ten Clay taught preschool for ten years in public schools in California, Missouri, and North Carolina and served as a Title IV preschool teacher consultant in Kansas City. For over twenty-five years she has served as a church preschool leader and also as a MOPS (Mothers of Preschoolers) volunteer. Ten Clay is coauthor of the preschool-kindergarten materials of the *LiFE* curriculum published by CRC Publications.

Van Ee is a professor and early childhood program advisor in the Education Department at Calvin College, Grand Rapids, Michigan. She has served as curriculum author and consultant for Christian Schools International and wrote the original Story Hour organization manual and curriculum materials for fours and fives.

Photo on page 5: Lori Adamski/Tony Stone Images; photo on page 20: Lawrence Monneret/Tony Stone Images.

Library of Congress Cataloging-in-Publication Data

Nederveld, Patricia L., 1944-
      Two coats for Joseph: the story of young Joseph/Patricia L. Nederveld.
         p. cm. — (God loves me; bk. 9)
      Summary: A simply retelling of how God took care of Joseph when his jealous brothers sold him into slavery in Egypt. Includes follow-up activities.
      ISBN 1-56212-278-9
      1. Joseph (Son of Jacob)—Juvenile literature. 2. Bible stories, English—O.T. Genesis. [1. Joseph (Son of Jacob) 2. Bible stories—O.T.] I. Title.
II. Series: Nederveld, Patricia L., 1944- God loves me; bk. 9.
BS580.J6N44 1998
222'.1109505—dc21
                                          97-37038
                                             CIP
                                           AC

10 9 8 7 6 5 4 3 2 1

Two Coats for Joseph
The Story of Young Joseph

PATRICIA L. NEDERVELD

ILLUSTRATIONS BY LISA WORKMAN

CRC Publications
Grand Rapids, Michigan

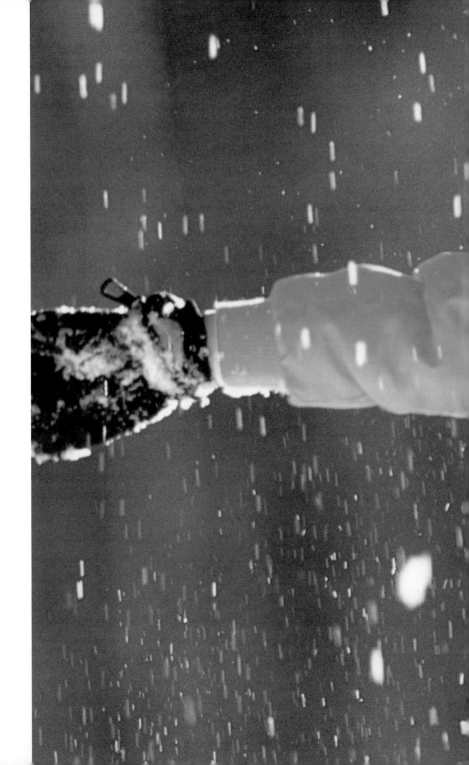

This is a story
from God's
book, the Bible.

It's for say name(s) of
your child(ren).
It's for me too!

Selections from
Genesis 37-41

Red, green,
blue, purple,
gold! What's
your favorite
color?

Joseph didn't have to choose just one color! His father gave him a wonderful new coat of amazing colors. Joseph loved wearing his coat.

But Joseph's brothers weren't a bit happy. "Our father loves Joseph best," they whispered to each other. They began to hate Joseph.

One day, when their father wasn't watching, Joseph's brothers grabbed him. They took away his colorful coat and threw Joseph into a deep, dark hole.

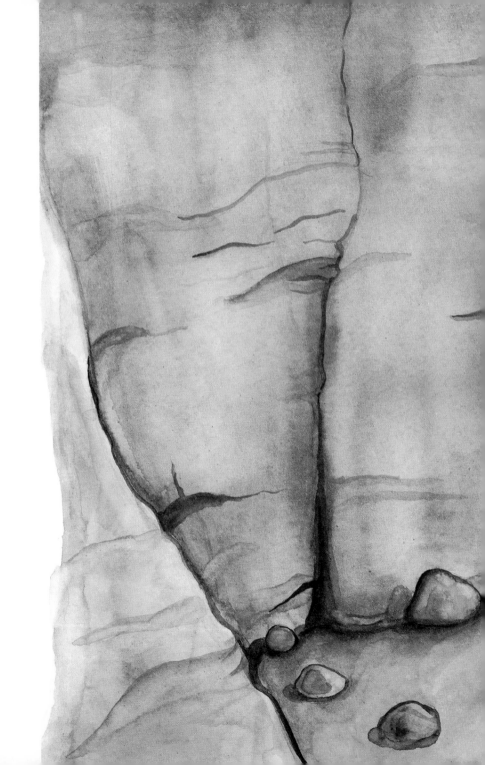

Do you think Joseph felt frightened, sitting alone at the bottom of that hole? Do you think he remembered that God was there with him, taking care of him?

At last Joseph's brothers pulled him out of the hole. But they didn't give his coat back. Instead, they sent Joseph far away to a strange land. Do you think Joseph remembered that God was going with him, taking good care of him?

A wonderful thing happened to Joseph in that faraway land. God brought Joseph to the palace of the great Pharaoh. God told Joseph just what to say to Pharaoh too. And Pharaoh was so amazed at the things Joseph told him that he chose Joseph to do a very important job.

Pharaoh gave Joseph a beautiful new coat to wear. He put a gold chain around Joseph's neck. People could see that Joseph was a great and important ruler.

And wherever Joseph went, he remembered that God was there with him, loving him and taking care of him. More than anything else, that made Joseph happy.

wonder if you know that wherever you are, God is there too, taking care of you . . .

Dear God, we're glad that wherever we are, you are there too. Thank you for always taking care of us. Amen.

Suggestions for Follow-up

Opening

Invite someone to play "God Is So Good" (Songs Section, *God Loves Me* program guide) on the piano, keyboard, or guitar as your little ones arrive. Welcome each one and express your delight that God has taken good care of each one this week.

As you begin today, celebrate God's goodness. Encourage children to mimic your words and actions:

> *We belong to God. Hurray!* (clap twice)
> *Thank you, God, for this fine day.* (fold hands as in prayer)
> *Hurray! Hurray!* (clap twice and then twice again)

You might substitute "God cares for us" for the first line and repeat the second and third lines again.

Learning Through Play

Learning through play is the best way! The following activity suggestions are meant to help you provide props and experiences that will invite the children to play their way into the Scripture story and its simple truth. Try to provide plenty of time for the children to choose their own activities and to play individually. Use group activities sparingly—little ones learn most comfortably with a minimum of structure.

1. Provide colorfully designed shirts, bath towels to use as a robe's train, a tinfoil crown, and gold chains for children to dress up like Joseph. Use clothespins to pin the bath towel around a child's neck so that it will slip off easily if pulled. As children try on the garments, help identify what part of the story is being shown. For example, say, "Oh, Joseph, your father just gave you that new coat! It's beautiful!" or "Look, Joseph, the king has made you his helper, and God is still taking care of you."

2. Invite your little ones to make a "hug" in your art center. Beforehand, cut strips of paper about 3-4" (10 cm) wide and about 3' (1 m) long. Write the caption God Is Always with Me along the strip of paper. Then help them trace around their hands—one on each end of the strip of paper. Show the children how to wrap the strip around them—like a hug from God!

3. Take time to sing "God Is So Good" (Songs Section, *God Loves Me* program guide) together. Try adding these new stanzas:

    > *He cares for me . . .*
    > *God loves me so . . .*

4. Beforehand, prepare crowns for each child from yellow posterboard using Pattern B (see Patterns Section, *God Loves Me* program guide). Or cut a sheet of yellow construction paper in half the long way, and tape the pieces together to form a long strip. Write the caption God Cares for Me on the strip. Provide crayons and sidewalk chalk for your little ones to decorate the crowns. If you wish, use a glue stick to add glitter or small paper shapes, or provide a variety of stickers.

5. Invite your little ones to scribble color on the sides of large paper bags with crayons or sidewalk chalk. When they've finished coloring, cut a slit up the center back of the bag. Cut a circle about 6" (15 cm) in diameter for the neck. Working from the inside of the bag, cut a half circle in the folded narrow sides of the bag for armholes. Help your little designers put on the colorful coats. Trim the cut edges a bit larger if necessary, and fold back the edges near the neck into lapels. Admire everyone's beautiful coat, and talk about how excited Joseph was about his new coat.

6. Collect several boxes large enough to hold one or two children. For safety, remove lids or flaps on the open end. You might want to cut windows or doors in some of the boxes. Encourage your little ones to enjoy pretending the boxes are cars or buses, or beds or houses, or . . . (Older children may want to pretend they are in the dark hole with Joseph or in the palace.) As they play, ask questions such as, "Where are you? Is God with you?" Remind them that God is always with us.

Closing

As you gather up the treasures of the day, talk about where everyone will go when they leave. Pray the prayer on page 21. Give each child a closing blessing, placing your hand on their heads as you remind them that God goes with them everywhere.

At Home

Little children learn through repetition. Take every opportunity to say over and over, "God is with you everywhere!" Play a question-and-answer game, asking, "Is God with you in (or at)_____?" Encourage your child to respond, "Yes, Hurray!" Clap as your child responds each time. Your little one is beginning to develop a sense of trust in God—you are a model of the heavenly Father's care.

Old Testament Stories

Blue and Green and Purple Too! *The Story of God's Colorful World*

It's a Noisy Place! *The Story of the First Creatures*

Adam and Eve *The Story of the First Man and Woman*

Take Good Care of My World! *The Story of Adam and Eve in the Garden*

A Very Sad Day *The Story of Adam and Eve's Disobedience*

A Rainy, Rainy Day *The Story of Noah*

Count the Stars! *The Story of God's Promise to Abraham and Sarah*

A Girl Named Rebekah *The Story of God's Answer to Abraham*

Two Coats for Joseph *The Story of Young Joseph*

Plenty to Eat *The Story of Joseph and His Brothers*

Safe in a Basket *The Story of Baby Moses*

I'll Do It! *The Story of Moses and the Burning Bush*

Safe at Last! *The Story of Moses and the Red Sea*

What Is It? *The Story of Manna in the Desert*

A Tall Wall *The Story of Jericho*

A Baby for Hannah *The Story of an Answered Prayer*

Samuel! Samuel! *The Story of God's Call to Samuel*

Lions and Bears! *The Story of David the Shepherd Boy*

David and the Giant *The Story of David and Goliath*

A Little Jar of Oil *The Story of Elisha and the Widow*

One, Two, Three, Four, Five, Six, Seven! *The Story of Elisha and Naaman*

A Big Fish Story *The Story of Jonah*

Lions, Lions! *The Story of Daniel*

New Testament Stories

Jesus Is Born! *The Story of Christmas*

Good News! *The Story of the Shepherds*

An Amazing Star! *The Story of the Wise Men*

Waiting, Waiting, Waiting! *The Story of Simeon and Anna*

Who Is This Child? *The Story of Jesus in the Temple*

Follow Me! *The Story of Jesus and His Twelve Helpers*

The Greatest Gift *The Story of Jesus and the Woman at the Well*

A Father's Wish *The Story of Jesus and a Little Boy*

Just Believe! *The Story of Jesus and a Little Girl*

Get Up and Walk! *The Story of Jesus and a Man Who Couldn't Walk*

A Little Lunch *The Story of Jesus and a Hungry Crowd*

A Scary Storm *The Story of Jesus and a Stormy Sea*

Thank You, Jesus! *The Story of Jesus and One Thankful Man*

A Wonderful Sight! *The Story of Jesus and a Man Who Couldn't See*

A Better Thing to Do *The Story of Jesus and Mary and Martha*

A Lost Lamb *The Story of the Good Shepherd*

Come to Me! *The Story of Jesus and the Children*

Have a Great Day! *The Story of Jesus and Zacchaeus*

I Love You, Jesus! *The Story of Mary's Gift to Jesus*

Hosanna! *The Story of Palm Sunday*

The Best Day Ever! *The Story of Easter*

Goodbye—for Now *The Story of Jesus' Return to Heaven*

A Prayer for Peter *The Story of Peter in Prison*

Sad Day, Happy Day! *The Story of Peter ad Dorcas*

A New Friend *The Story of Paul's Conversion*

Over the Wall *The Story of Paul's Escape in a Basket*

A Song in the Night *The Story of Paul and Silas in Prison*

A Ride in the Night *The Story of Paul's Escape on Horseback*

The Shipwreck *The Story of Paul's Rescue at Sea*

Holiday Stories

Selected stories from the New Testament to help you celebrate the Christian year

Jesus Is Born! *The Story of Christmas*

Good News! *The Story of the Shepherds*

An Amazing Star! *The Story of the Wise Men*

Hosanna! *The Story of Palm Sunday*

The Best Day Ever! *The Story of Easter*

Goodbye—for Now *The Story of Jesus' Return to Heaven*

These fifty-two books are the heart of *God Loves Me*, a Bible story program designed for young children. Individual books (or the entire set) and the accompanying program guide *God Loves Me* are available from CRC Publications (1-800-333-8300).

Two Coats for Joseph tells the story of young Joseph (found in Genesis 37-41) in simple words a young child can understand. Beautiful illustrations help little ones learn about God's love. Suggestions for follow-up provide creative ideas to help children respond to the Bible story with their mouths and eyes and ears—and hands and feet too!

This Bible storybook is one of fifty-two books in the *God Loves Me* series for young children.

CRC Publications
ISBN 1-56212-278-9

A Little Jar of Oil
The Story of Elisha and the Widow

PATRICIA L. NEDERVELD